MONSTER INSECTS
OF THE MOVIES
By John LeMay

Copyright © 2020 by Bicep Books.

All images reproduced within this book derive from memorabilia, publicity photos, and other publicity materials. This material appears here for the sole purpose of publicity and education. The publisher also wishes to acknowledge that they claim no rights to the underlying artistic works, photos, or images embodied in this book.

MONSTER INSECTS
OF THE MOVIES

Behind the scenes of the classic bug movie Them! *(1954).*

CREEPY CRAWLIES

Bugs have made people's skin crawl since the dawn of time. Therefore it's no surprise that insects appear in horror and sci-fi movies. Even though small bugs can be creepy enough, it's the giant bugs that have fascinated moviegoers since the 1950s. The premise of some of these films, like 1957's *The Deadly Mantis*, focused on giant prehistoric bugs revived in the modern era. While there were no giant praying mantises, as seen in the film, there were such things as Meganuera, giant dragonflies. There were even a few giant centipedes—but sorry, no giant ants, mantises, or spiders like the ones seen in the movies.

But when did people start using giant bugs as the antagonists in horror stories and films? The answer might surprise you. The first story on record was an old newspaper hoax from 1894 entitled "The Monster of Issoire." The story, written as though it really happened, took place in France. Over several nights in the spring of 1894, several people had mysteriously disappeared. One night a policeman heard a mysterious kind of music coming from the catacombs and decided to follow it. At the source of the music was a dog-sized spider feeding on one of its victims! The story ended with the policeman shooting the monster dead, and stated that the body would be put on display at the Museum of Natural History. Of course, it never was. Nor did the story explain the connection between the spider and the music. Still, it would have made for a great horror movie…

Next, in the 1930s, a hoaxed story (backed up by fake photographs) appeared about giant grasshoppers! Many people believed the photos to be real, and postcards featuring the images sold "like hotcakes."

Rare surviving still from the "Spider Pit" scene from King Kong *(1933).*

The first cinematic giant bugs should have debuted in the 1933 classic *King Kong*. The film had a famous deleted scene where sailors from the *Venture* fell into a gorge inhabited by all sorts of giant spiders and insects. Supposedly, the scene was so horrific that audiences of the time couldn't handle it, and so it was removed from the film. Today many film historians still wonder if we will ever unearth the lost "spider pit sequence" as it is now called.

Thanks to this, giant bugs didn't make their big-screen debut until over twenty years later in 1954's *Them!* The movie was a big hit and is considered by many to be the definitive giant bug movie. Something you may not know about *Them!* was that it was originally supposed to be shot in 3-D and color! At the last minute, the studio, Warners Bros, decided to keep things simple by shooting it in black and white instead.

Them! opens in the New Mexico desert, not far from where the first atomic bomb was tested in 1945. Wandering across the dunes is a little girl all alone. She is rescued by two policemen, Peterson and Blackburn, who discover she belongs to a family that went missing recently while on vacation in the area.

Eventually, giant ants mutated by the atomic bomb tests are discovered to be the culprits behind the disappearances and deaths. To investigate, the FBI sends Special Agent Robert Graham along with Dr. Harold Medford of the Department of Agriculture. With him is his daughter, Dr. Pat Medford.

Together the trio finds the nest of the giant ants, and cyanide gas bombs are dropped inside to exterminate the creatures. However, Graham, Peterson, and Pat explore the den and discover that two queen ants have survived to create new colonies elsewhere.

Some of the exciting action in **Them!**

Soon reports come in of a pilot being forced to land by UFOs that looked like giant ants. Then the Coast Guard receives word of the giant queen attacking a freighter at sea in the Pacific. The report of a huge sugar theft in Los Angeles leads Peterson, Graham, and Pat there to investigate. It is soon learned that the ants have established a new colony within the Los Angeles River drainage channel. The military attacks the ants, and in the chaos, Peterson rescues two boys that had become trapped within the nest. The rest of the ant eggs are destroyed with flamethrowers. When the smoke clears, one of the characters proclaims, "When Man entered the Atomic Age, he opened the door to a new world. What we may eventually find in that new world, nobody can predict."

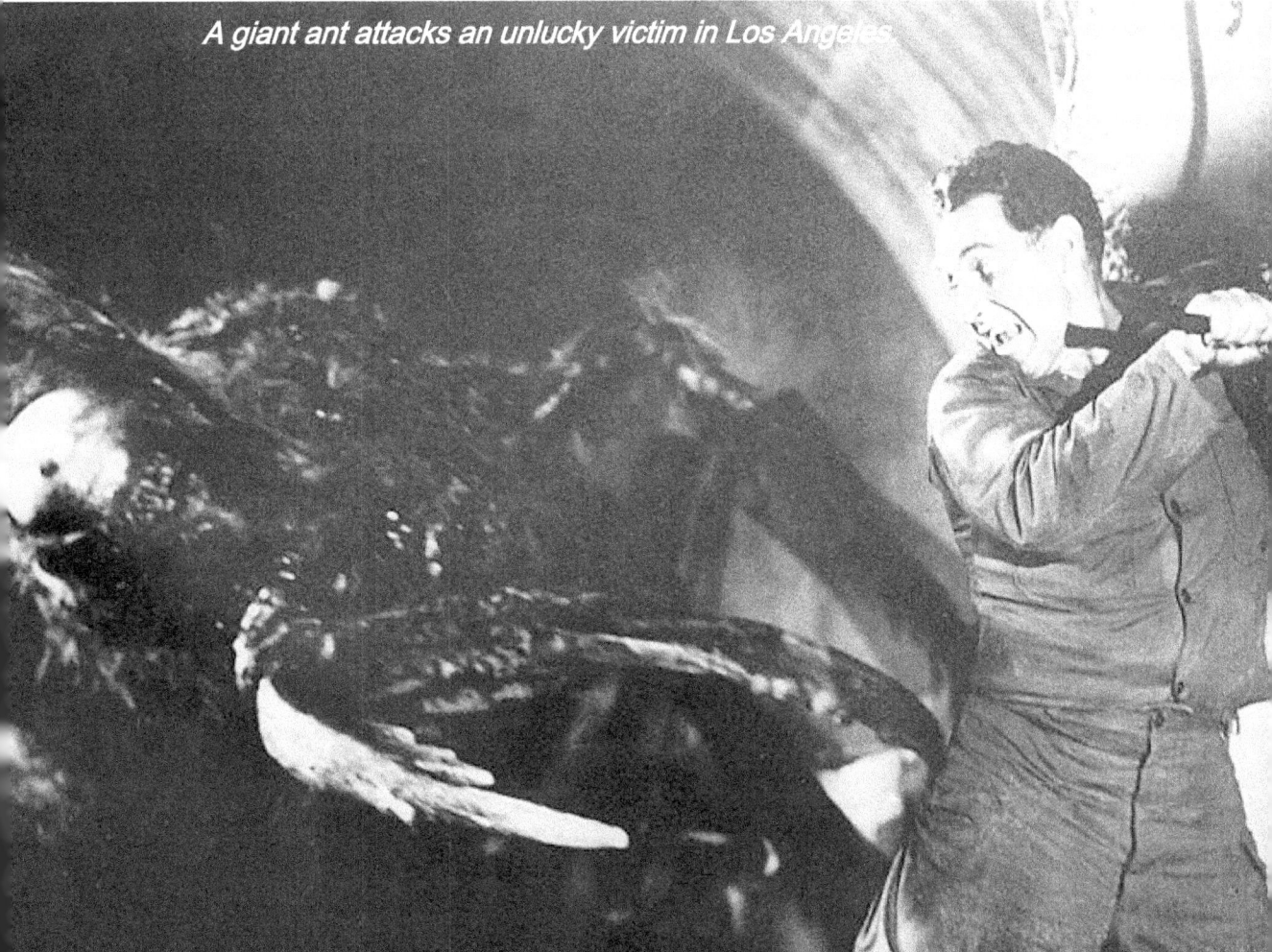

A giant ant attacks an unlucky victim in Los Angeles.

Due to the success of *Them!*, next came *Tarantula!* the very next year in 1955. Similar to *Them!*, the original idea for *Tarantula* was for a movie about a horde of giant spiders. But, instead of a group of moderately large spiders, someone decided instead to do a story about one truly mammoth spider.

Actress Mara Corday recoils in fear in Tarantula! *(1955).*

From right to left, actors John Agar, Leo Carroll, and Mara Corday.

Tarantula! begins with a strange, deformed man wandering through the Arizona desert. Dr. Matt Hastings investigates the peculiar case. In doing so, he picks up the trail of the eccentric Dr. Gerald Deemer and his assistant Stephanie Clayton. In secret, Dr. Deemer has been developing a new type of super nutrient with radiation. This was the cause of the deformed man. But what's worse is that Dr. Deemer has been using the super nutrient on various animals to make them grow larger, including a tarantula. One night, a disgruntled worker of Deemer's sets the lab on fire, and the giant tarantula escapes. The giant arachnid goes on a killing spree, eating humans and animals alike, leaving behind no witnesses. Dr. Hastings finds a strange sub-

Tarantula! *publicity still.*

stance left behind at one of the kill sites and finds it to be tarantula venom.

Soon the giant tarantula makes itself known to the public when it attacks Deemer's mansion, killing him, though Stephanie escapes. The tarantula marches on the nearby town, with bullets from police rifles failing to harm the giant bug. Even dynamite fails to stop its progress. Finally, a squadron of jet fighters put the monster down right on the town line.

Still from **The Beginning of the End** *(1957).*

The next big bug movie to hit theaters was about giant locusts and was titled *The Beginning of the End*. Inspired by *Them!* and the H.G. Wells novel, *Food of the Gods*, the story concerned locusts that had eaten crops grown with radiation. As such, the insects grow to giant size and go on a rampage.

To bring the big bugs to life, stop-motion animation was considered but was decided to be too costly and time-consuming. Therefore the director, Burt I. Gordon, simply used rear projection shots of real grasshoppers mixed in with photographs of various buildings.

When the creatures invade Chicago, authorities consider dropping an atom bomb on them. But, at the last moment, a scientist devises a plant to lure the locusts to the cold waters of Lake Michigan, where the cold water will render the bugs immobile. Using a fake locust call, the insects travel to the lake, and the plan works. The movie ends with scientists wondering what other giant animals the irradiated crops might have created…

Cut from the same cloth as *Tarantula!* was *The Deadly Mantis*. In this case, rather than being mutated by radiation, the titular monster is simply a prehistoric species of giant mantis frozen in the Arctic. Actually, in the original script, the prehistoric mantis was released from its icy prison due to nuclear testing, but this was changed to a volcanic eruption for fear that this would upset the U.S. military, whose cooperation was needed to produce the picture. The whole movie was shot in only 13 days. After filming was over, producers decided to add in one more scene where the mantis climbs the Washington Monument.

Scene from the ending of *The Deadly Mantis*.

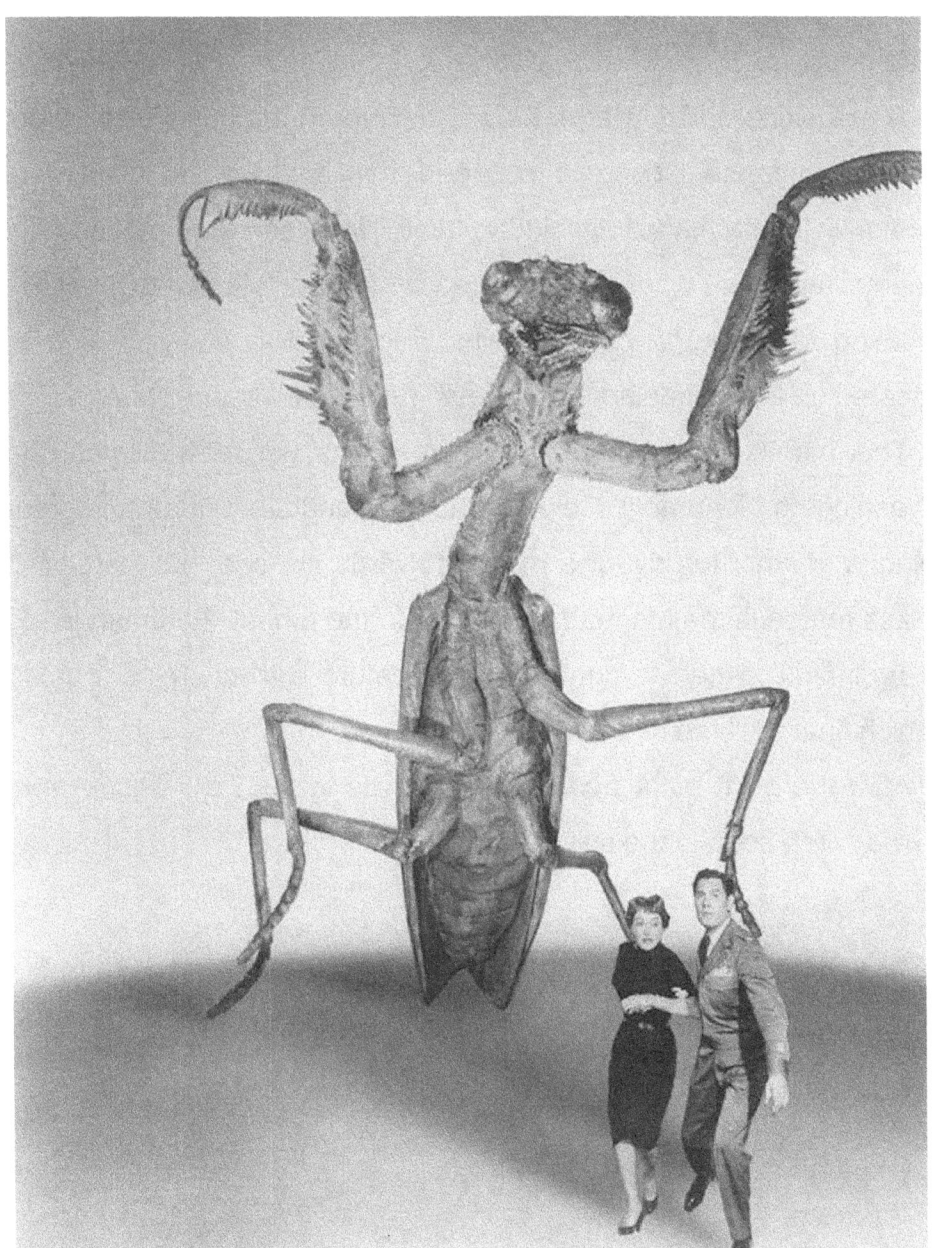

The Deadly Mantis kicks off with a 200-foot-long praying mantis being freed from its icy tomb. Soon after, an outpost in the Arctic is mysteriously destroyed. Leading an investigation is Colonel Joe Parkman, who discovers a strange fragment amidst the wreckage. Eventually, a paleontologist, Dr. Nedrick Jackson, identifies it as a piece of a prehistoric praying mantis!

A magazine editor, Marge Blaine, gets in on the investigation too, and a romance blossoms between her and Colonel Parkman. Meanwhile, the mantis attacks an Inuit village and then moves onto the military base where it is spotted by Marge. Man's weapons do nothing to the huge creature which simply flies away. It is next located off the Canadian Coast, heading for the United States.

The mantis lands in Washington, D.C., where it climbs the Washington Monument. Colonel Parkman and a squadron of fighter planes attempt to drive the mantis towards the sea, but instead, it takes refuge in the Manhattan Tunnel. In the tunnel, Parkman leads a regiment of men to confront the creature with chemical bombs which finally kill the mantis.

After the giant mantis came giant wasps in 1957's *Monster from Green Hell*, seen in the still below.

The "Monster from Green Hell" is created when wasps are sent into outer space in a rocket. Scientists are using animals in experiments to see how being in space affects earth-based life-forms. The test backfires when the wasps become mutated by cosmic radiation and crash to earth in Africa. Soon reports come in of giant flying monsters there, and scientists are sent to investigate. The lead scientist speculates that if the queen wasp is destroyed, then the whole colony will perish. Explosives are planted within a volcano to induce an eruption, and the lava kills the giant wasps.

The monster from Green Hell catches its dinner.

In 1957, a giant spider had a significant cameo in *The Incredible Shrinking Man*. The classic sci-fi script penned by Richard Matheson focused on a man named Scott who began to shrink after being exposed to a radiation cloud at sea. Over the course of the movie, Scott shrinks down to the size of a child and eventually becomes so small that his pet cat tries to eat him. Scott becomes lost in the basement of his home, where his main adversary is a spider—gigantic to the tiny Scott. Eventually, Scott kills the spider, but the film doesn't exactly have a happy ending. There is no cure for Scott, who will continue to shrink until he enters the subatomic level.

Exciting still from **The Incredible Shrinking Man** *(1957).*

Humorous publicity still for The Monster That Challenged the World.

In 1957 also came *The Monster That Challenged the World*. Don't let the publicity still above, taken as a joke, fool you. The hideous monster mollusk was a terror to everyone in the film, which ends with the monstrosity exterminated by the military.

Giant bugs continued to fill movie screens in 1957, and next up was *The Black Scorpion*. After all, with giant ants and spiders getting so much attention, it was only natural that scorpions would be next! As a bonus, in addition to the main antagonists, *The Black Scorpion* also contained giant worms and spiders.

The Black Scorpion's premise is similar to *The Deadly Mantis* in that it kicks off with a volcanic eruption awakening prehistoric bugs. In this case, all the action takes place in a Mexican village, San Lorenzo, where geologists arrive to study the new volcano. They find more than they bargained for when cattle begin to die mysteriously. The culprits are revealed to be prehistoric giant scorpions that live within the volcano. Eventually, the scorpions descend on the village and the Mexican military is powerless to stop them. When the scorpions return to the cave from which they came, the heroes dynamite the entrance sealing them in.

Some of the other giant bugs from **The Black Scorpion** *(1957).*

The Black Scorpion itself.

However, the dynamiting of the cave doesn't prove to be the picture's end. The scorpions get out again, and in a famous scene derail a train. The massive scorpions then begin to fight each other until only one remains. The biggest surviving scorpion heads for Mexico City. The heroes devise a plan to lure it to a stadium with a truckload of meat. As the military distracts the monster, the hero shoots it with a spear with an electric cable attached to it.

The special effects for *The Black Scorpion* were done by none other than Willis O'Brien, the animator behind *The Lost World* (1925) and *King Kong* (1933). In fact, some sources even say *The Black Scorpion's* giant spider was the same model used in *King Kong's* lost Spider Pit scene!

Still from **The Strange World of Planet X** *(1958).*

The Strange World of Planet X, released in 1958, combined the worlds of aliens from outer space and giant bugs. In this case, the aliens were friendly, and came to warn against the experiments of an earth man that created a giant spider.

Next up was another more traditional spider movie like *Tarantula!* entitled *Earth vs. the Spider* (1958). The story kicks off with the search for a missing man, who disappeared the night of his daughter Carol's birthday. Carol and her boyfriend Mike find her father's wrecked car next to an old cave. Thinking he may have crawled inside, they go in to explore. There they fall into the web of a giant spider and narrowly avoid being eaten!

The authorities don't believe the teenagers' wild story until they receive the assistance of their science teacher, Mr. Kingman, who finds the body of Carol's father drained of all fluids. The spider emerges to attack the exploration party, which includes the sheriff. The lawmen use DDT to kill the big bug, and its seemingly lifeless body is brought back to town where it is displayed in the school gym.

Publicity still from Earth vs. the Spider.

Rock 'n' Roll music from a band revives the monster, and it goes on a rampage through the town before returning to its cave. The sheriff dynamites the cave, not knowing that Carol and Mike are inside. Kingman then gets a few electrodes from the power company and attaches them to the spider's web, electrocuting it and causing it to fall onto a stalagmite.

Though the movie's title card does read as "Earth vs. the Spider," when it came time to release the film, the title was shortened to simply "The Spider" due to the success that same year of *The Fly*.

People fleeing from Earth vs. the Spider's *title character.*

Vincent Price and his co-star in The Fly *(1958).*

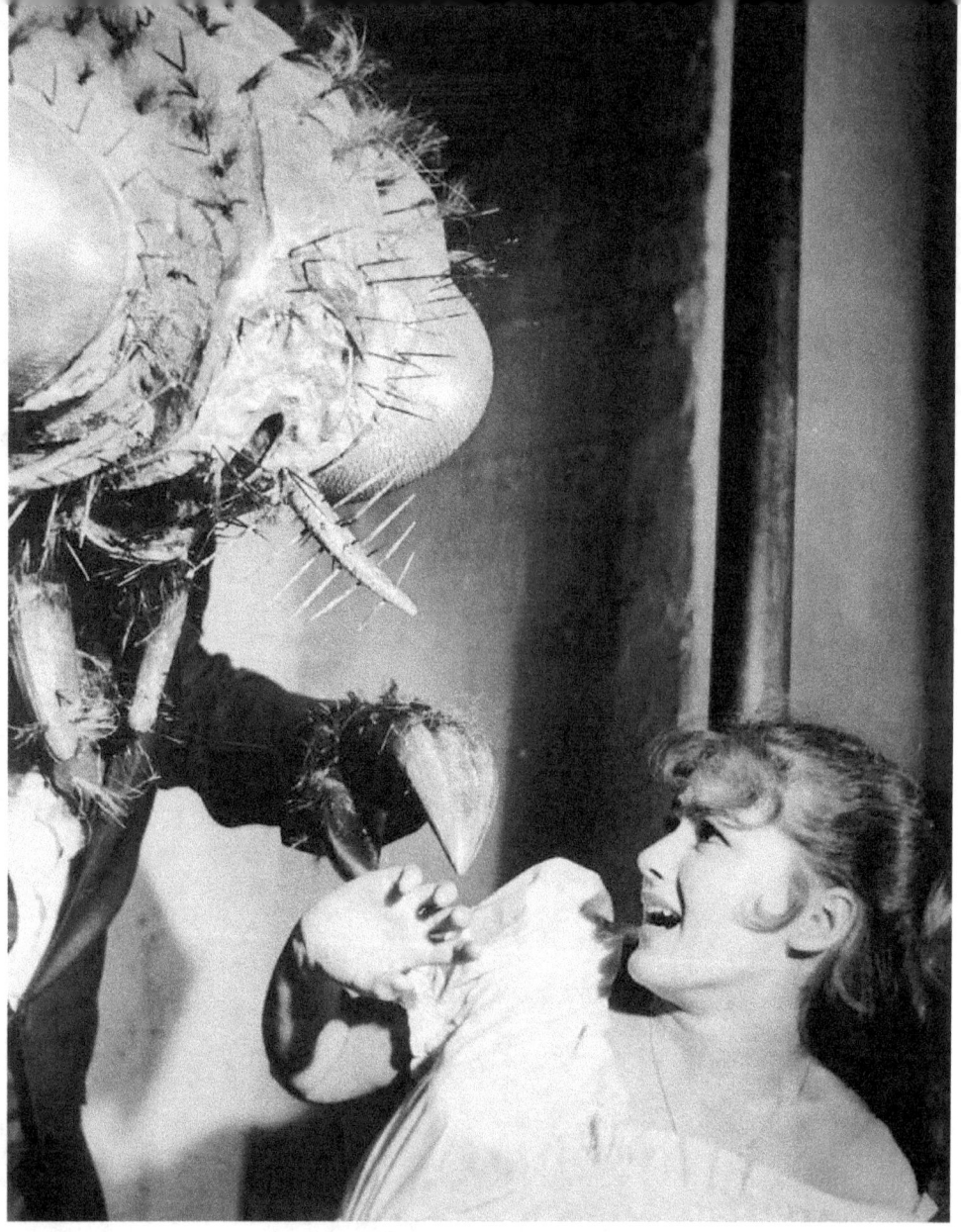

Still from The Fly *(1958).*

The Fly was the first movie to combine a human and an insect. Actually, it was one of the first movies in which scientific experiments combined people and animals, and would lead to similar movies like *The Alligator People* the next year. *The Fly* was a huge success with one critic stating that it was "the most ludicrous, and certainly one of the most revolting science-horror films ever perpetrated."

The Fly focuses on André Delambre (Al Hedison), who has created a machine that can transport matter from one spot to the next called the disintegrator-integrator. Andre tests the machine on himself, but unknown to him, a fly has entered the transportation chamber. Andre flips the switch and comes out with the head and arm of a fly, while the fly has his head and arm on it!

Ashamed to show his face to his wife Hélène (Patricia Owens), he hides it under a cloth but tells her the truth. To reverse the process, they need to find the elusive fly with his head and arm. But the tiny fly is never found and André decides to end his life with the assistance of Hélène, who is almost arrested for what appears to be a murder. But, at the last second, Andre's brother François (Vincent Price) finds the elusive fly and shows it to the head detective, Charas (Herbert Marshall). Charas crushes the abomination and declares Andre's death a suicide to free Hélène from the charges.

Vincent Price returned for a sequel, *Return of the Fly*, the very next year, reprising his role as François. The story is set years later, when Andre's grown son Phillipe (Brett Halsey) continues his father's experiments, hoping to succeed where his father had failed. As you can guess, an accident turns Phillipe into a fly monster just like his father. But, there's a twist. Phillipe is knocked out by industrial spies and placed in the matter teleportation chamber with a fly on purpose. Phillipe awakens as a fly man and then tracks down the men who wronged him. Phillipe kills the men and, unlike the first film, is restored to his human form at the picture's end.

Still from The Wasp Woman *(1959) starring Susan Cabot.*

The success of *The Fly* inspired an imitator, *The Wasp Woman*, in 1959. The film was produced by Roger Corman and centered on the owner of a large cosmetics company, Janice Starlin, who becomes concerned when her sales begin to drop. Starlin teams with a scientist, Dr. Eric Zinthrop, who believes he can create an anti-aging serum from the royal jelly of a queen wasp. Janice serves as the doctor's test subject, taking doses of the serum. However, when it doesn't produce the desired results, she sneaks into his lab one night and injects herself with extra doses. It works, and Janice reverses her own aging process. But there's a horrible side effect as Janice eventually begins to take on the physical traits of a wasp and becomes violent. At the picture's end, Zinthrop throws carbolic acid in her face and she falls out of a window!

The next giant bugs to terrorize the silver screen were hideous leeches in *Attack of the Giant Leeches*. Shot in a little over one week, *Attack of the Giant Leeches* tells the story of—you guessed it—giant leeches created from radiation. The creatures drag their victims to an underwater cavern to slowly feed on them until the heroes dynamite the cave, sealing the monsters inside.

RETURN OF THE GIANT BUGS

After a spat of films in the 1950s concluding with *Attack of the Giant Leeches*, giant bugs disappeared from movie screens… in America that is. In Japan, several special effects studios had picked up the slack. In 1957 Toho produced *Rodan*, a movie about a giant pterodactyl that begins with giant bugs emerging from a mine. Next, Daiei studios shot *The Invisible Man vs. the Human Fly*, a movie that was never released in America. In 1961 came the most famous bug monster of all, *Mothra*, about a benevolent butterfly that protects two tiny fairies. Mothra would go on to battle Godzilla in *Godzilla vs. the Thing* (1964). Later, the big bug would ally with Godzilla to battle the title character in *Ghidrah, the Three-Headed Monster* (1965), and a giant shrimp in *Godzilla Versus the Sea Monster* (1968). In 1969, Godzilla also battled Spiega, a giant spider, and giant praying mantises in *Son of Godzilla*. Mothra, the giant mantises, and Spiega would all return for *Destroy All Monsters* (1969) and *Godzilla's Revenge* (1970). Godzilla continues to battle big bugs to this day in movies like *Godzilla vs. Megalon* (1976), in which he fought a giant beetle, Megalon, and a robot, Gigan. The strange robot monster Gigan returned for *Godzilla on Monster Island* (1978), where it and Ghidrah are controlled by alien cockroaches!

In the U.S., big bug movies made a comeback after the success of *Jaws*, beginning with *Bug* in 1975 about prehistoric cockroaches. The cockroaches, which can breathe fire, are all exterminated but one. A scientist then crossbreeds the prehistoric roach with the modern variety, creating an even more dealy pest!

Joan Collins in Empire of the Ants *(1977).*

The Giant Spider Invasion also came out in 1975 and featured aliens spiders! A meteorite crashes to earth, heralding the arrival of monstrous spiders of various sizes, which are all reduced to goo in the end when the scientist heroes drain the alien arachnids of their energy.

The giant spider was brought to life with a Volkswagen car covered with black fur and fake spider legs, which were operated from within the vehicle by seven members of the crew. The car's red tail lights even served as the giant spider's glowing eyes!

Publicity still for *The Giant Spider Invasion with a painted-in spider.*

Kingdom of the Spiders came out in 1977 and starred *Star Trek's* William Shatner as a veterinarian in rural Verde Valley, Arizona, investigating cattle mutilations. Shatner's character, Dr. Hansen, unravels the mystery when he takes blood samples from a dead calf and discovers extremely high traces of spider venom. Hansen teams with Diane Ashley, an arachnologist, and discovers a huge spider den near where the animal was killed.

Soon an army of spiders besieges Verde Valley cutting the town off from the outside world. Though the spiders never grow gigantic, they use their excessive numbers to their advantage to overwhelm the city. Hansen, Ashley, and other survivors barricade themselves inside of a lodge. When it becomes evident that no one is coming to save them, Hansen decides to go outside to get help. To his horror, the entire town is covered in spider webbing and the movie ends.

Exciting still from Empire of the Ants *(1977)*.

The last great bug movie in recent years, like the first, was another giant ant movie: 1977's *Empire of the Ants*. The film starred future *Dynasty* actress Joan Collins as a crooked land developer who is taking some clients on a tour of new beachfront property on an island. The area is also the site of a toxic chemical spill that has mutated the ant population into giant monsters.

Collins' character, Marilyn Fryser, and her clients soon become stranded on the island when the ants destroy their boat and chase them into the swamps of the island. The survivors think they have found hope when they see a nearby town. But, the situation is even worse than they imagined. The ants aren't just mindless monsters; the queen ant is using pheromones to mind control the human population! In doing so, the populace provides the ants with sugar from a local factory. Though Fryser ends up dying, one of the heroes drives a gas tank into the sugar factory, blowing up most of the ants.

He and the other three survivors then find a new boat to escape the island.

Empire of the Ants was directed by Bert I. Gordon, who also made *The Beginning of the End*. Like that film, Gordon used real ants combined with miniatures and processed shots for the effects (in addition to a few giant ant props).

With modern blockbusters like *Jaws* and *Star Wars* having changed how we look at special effects, *Empire of the Ants* may well be the last giant bug movie made with the old special effects techniques. Time will tell if and when giant bugs crawl across the silver screen once more...

Joan Collins shares a laugh with her co-star.

Empire of the Ants *(1977)*.

THE BIG BOOK OF JAPANESE GIANT MONSTER MOVIES SERIES
VOLUME 1: 1954-1982
VOLUME 2: 1984-2017
THE LOST FILMS
TERROR OF THE LOST TOKUSATSU FILMS
WRITING JAPANESE MONSTERS
EDITING JAPANESE MONSTERS
KONG UNMADE: THE LOST FILMS OF SKULL ISLAND

Be sure to read these other great books!

www.ingramcontent.com/pod-product-compliance
Lightning Source LLC
Chambersburg PA
CBHW081237080526
44587CB00022B/3974